Hollywood Classics

CITIZEN KANE

Hollywood Classics

CITIZEN KANE

Lynne Piade

SMITHMARK
PUBLISHERS INC.

Published by Smithmark Publishers
112 Madison Avenue
New York, New York 10016

Produced by
Brompton Books Corp.
15 Sherwood Place
Greenwich, CT 06830

ISBN 0-8317-4573-8

Printed in Hong Kong

10 9 8 7 6 5 4 3 2 1

Designed by Tom Debolski

All photos appear courtesy of American Graphic
Systems Picture Archive with the following
exceptions:
Brompton Books Picture Archive 36-37, 47
Indiana University/ Lilly Library 25, 29, 60, 61
The Museum of Modern Art/Film Stills Archive
  102-103
State Historical Society of Wisconsin/Blum Theater
  Collection 100-101
Wisconsin Center for Film & Theater Research 17, 24,
  30, 46

Page 1: On the eve of the election, a cocky Charlie Kane gives a rousing campaign speech as the Independent candidate for governor.

Page 2: An uncredited photo of Orson Welles as a middle-aged Charles Foster Kane in his monumental film, **Citizen Kane**.

CITIZEN KANE

CAST

Charles Foster Kane	Orson Welles
Jedediah Leland	Joseph Cotten
Susan Alexander Kane	Dorothy Comingore
Kane's mother	Agnes Moorehead
Emily Norton Kane	Ruth Warrick
James W Gettys	Ray Collins
Mr Carter	Erskine Sanford
Mr Bernstein	Everett Sloane
Thompson, the reporter	William Alland
Walter Parks Thatcher	George Coulouris

Director-Producer	Orson Welles
Screenplay	Herman J Mankiewicz
	Orson Welles
	(with the assistance of Joseph Cotten and John Houseman)
Director of Photography	Gregg Toland, ASC
Editor	Robert Wise
	(and Mark Robson)
Score	Bernard Herrmann

INTRODUCTION

The film opens with the last few minutes in the life of newspaper magnate Charles Foster Kane. The camera slowly pans down the fence surrounding Kane's palatial estate, Xanadu, and at last settles upon a 'No Trespassing' sign. Inside this forbidding exterior, Charles Foster Kane is alone. In his hand is a glass paperweight with a winter scene inside it. In the dying man's last breath he utters a single word: 'Rosebud.' The paperweight falls to the ground, bounces once and shatters.

What does 'Rosebud' mean and why would it be the last word on Kane's lips? Aspiring to offer a neat conclusion to his newsreel on Kane's life, a reporter hopes to solve the enigma that is Kane by uncovering the answers to these questions.

Citizen Kane is viewed as a milestone in the development of cinematic technique. Written by Orson Welles and Herman J Mankiewicz with the assistance of Joseph Cotten and John Houseman, **Citizen Kane** has earned praise on many fronts. In 1942 it won the New York Film Critics Award and at the Academy Awards, Welles and Mankiewicz shared an Oscar for Best Original Screenplay. Three decades later in 1971, *Sight and Sound*, a leading British film quarterly, called **Citizen Kane** the greatest film ever made. In 1989 the Library of Congress honored **Citizen Kane**, citing the film's cultural, historical and artistic impact on American film history.

The story of Citizen Kane himself unfolds before our eyes through the recollections of four people who were close to him: Kane's best friend, Leland; his ex-wife, Susan; his personal manager, Bernstein; and finally his butler, Raymond. A fifth testimony is found in the memoirs of Walter Parks Thatcher, Kane's legal guardian and later bank manager. Through multiple flashbacks and a series of tightly woven vignettes, each person provides a fascinating, though individually incomplete, picture of Charles Foster Kane.

Right: A promotional still of director Orson Welles on the set of **Citizen Kane**.

Welles' deviation from heretofore traditional linear narrative structure, a technique not uncommon today, is perhaps the most striking and revolutionary aspect of this extremely innovative film. It is the unique treatment of biography that merits distinction here. Instead of a chronological history with a beginning, middle and end, we are given many distinct views of the same subject—Charles Foster Kane.

Together with the reporter, known to us only as 'Thompson,' we doggedly search for clues in the interviews to the meaning of the cryptic 'Rosebud'. None have the answer to what 'Rosebud' signifies and it is not until the drama's last few minutes of screen time that the meaning of 'Rosebud' is at last revealed. More a symbolic reference to lost innocence than the appraisal of a man's life, the word 'Rosebud' and the image of the child's burning sled leave an enduring and beautiful impression. It creates empathy in the hearts of the audience for Kane, a man who never expressed more than superficial emotions or felt deeply about anything.

Kane was an influential public figure who, 50 years earlier, had printed a 'Declaration of Principles' on the front page of his fledgling newspaper pledging that the *Inquirer* would print the truth. But the 'truth' took on the aspect of the truth according to Charlie Kane. Kane made his reputation as a wealthy champion of the underclasses who was not above creating news in order to sell more papers.

Citizen Kane was set to premiere on 14 February 1941 at the Radio City Music Hall. The Music Hall usually was the venue of choice for RKO film openings because it was partially owned by the Rockefellers and Chase National Bank, who also owned RKO.

Right: The 25-year-old Welles was at first unprepared for the demands of acting before a camera. Having acted on stage for many years and directed and produced radio broadcasts, he was an able director. However, with film, unlike live performance, it is *essential* that actors hit their chalk marks, and this was something that Welles found difficult to do. After completing his scenes during rehearsal he would ask for constructive criticism from the cast, gaining confidence in his ability to move before the camera. Sometimes he would watch another actor move through his own scene just to get an idea of what he looked like on film. In return, he would scrutinize the actors' movements and insist on perfection.

It has been assumed that Welles modelled the fictional character after the larger-than-life newspaper tycoon, William Randolph Hearst. Indeed, Hearst was so incensed by this portrayal, which he considered a parody, that he threatened to cripple the movie industry with bad publicity.

There were rumors that Hearst would retaliate by panning all RKO pictures and that the movie industry as a whole would suffer severely from **Citizen Kane**'s release.

Fearing the backlash, and the injury to his personal association with Hearst, Louis B Mayer, head of production at MGM, contacted Nicholas Schenk, the chairman of the board of Loew's International, the MGM affiliate in charge of distribution for MGM pictures. With Schenk as the middleman, Mayer offered George J Schaefer, president of RKO, the sum of $842,000 if Schaefer would destroy all existing prints and the negative of **Citizen Kane**. This payment would cover the $686,033 it cost RKO to make the film and included an additional $155,967 to cover the cost of post-production losses.

The $842,000 was looked upon as insurance by top movie magnates who contributed with Mayer to protect what they saw as their interests. They couldn't afford bad or no publicity for their movies or for their theaters in Hearst's newspapers and magazines nationwide. Few theaters would risk showing **Citizen Kane**, and it was limited to RKO-owned houses or small art theaters. Schaefer suspected that the company heads had struck a deal with Hearst and agreed not to show **Citizen Kane** in their theaters. Eventually Warners' broke with the pack and Fox, Paramount and Loew's followed half-heartedly.

By the time the film began showing at Warners' theaters, it was too late for financial success at the box office. In mid-1942 Schaefer, blamed for the damage to RKO's image and stock, left RKO. Two weeks later, Welles and his associates were ousted from the offices they had occupied on the RKO lot. Thereafter Welles was effectively punished with restricted directorial freedom on his succeeding projects.

Right: Joseph Cotten met Orson Welles in the winter of 1935. A soft-spoken, tall, young man, the 30-year-old Cotten played the part of Jedediah Leland in **Citizen Kane**.

Left: Ruth Warrick made her screen debut as Emily Norton Kane and worked with Orson Welles again in 1942 in the thriller **Journey into Fear**. During the 1940s she was one of Hollywood's leading ladies. Still in her longest running role, she today plays the part of Phoebe on the television soap opera series 'All My Children.'

Above: Ray Collins, a veteran of stage and radio, came to Hollywood with Orson Welles to play Boss Jim Gettys. He was also in Welles' **The Magnificent Ambersons** (1942). From 1957 to 1965 he played District Attorney Hamilton Burger in television's longest-running lawyer series, 'Perry Mason.'

Despite the scandal surrounding the film's release and the bitter taste the ordeal left in Welles' mouth, **Citizen Kane** far surpassed the goals its creators set regarding technical details. Welles' goal, to increase realism and make mechanical details imperceptible, was accomplished to a large extent with the remarkable talents of cameraman Gregg Toland and composer Bernard Herrmann. **Citizen Kane** was, for them both, their first foray into cinema. Despite their relative inexperience, they succeeded in producing an innovative and radical film for their day.

For example, many sequences in what is known as the 'breakfast montage' were cut by Welles to fit the musical score Herrmann had created, giving the score greater significance overall. In the final version of the montage, the music that complements the succession of six perfectly crafted scenes revealing the visual disintegration of Kane's first marriage, acts as the audio counterpoint of the montage. The imaginative Herrmann also wrote the excerpts of the fictitious French Oriental opera, *Salammbô*, for the scenes of Susan's operatic debut.

Striving for 'visual reality,' a term coined by Toland, the unconventional use of ceilinged sets was an attempt at authenticity that allowed for the placement of hidden microphones in the muslin of the ceiling, thereby eliminating the shadow cast by overhead mikes. It also allowed for natural lighting, giving the sets a more natural appearance, which effectively increased the sense of closeness and tension.

According to Gregg Toland, one of **Citizen Kane**'s greatest successes was 'fitting the photography to the story instead of limiting the story to the narrow confines of conventional photographic practice.' Both Welles and Toland shared the desire to attain an approximate human-eye focus, which Toland accomplished after weeks of preproduction testing. By using a shorter-focus wide-angle lens, the camera was able to hold sharp focus over a depth of 200 feet. This increased depth of field allowed for a flexible camera, liberating the movement of the camera's eye between the foreground and the background. Moreover, at the writing stage, the action from scene to scene was meticulously planned to avoid cuts, making transitions smooth.

Left: Dorothy Comingore played Kane's second wife, 'singer' Susan Alexander. After playing comedic roles with the Three Stooges and bit parts in low-grade Westerns in the mid-1930s, she got her big break in 1941 with **Citizen Kane**.

This technique was in line with Welles' well-known aversion to the close-up: 'I don't like to force it, and the use of the close-up amounts to forcing it: you can see nothing else.' In the entirety of **Citizen Kane**, Welles used fewer than a half-dozen close-ups. Such deliberate lack of a 'single viewpoint' has left many reviewers puzzled, not quite sure what they were *supposed* to see. Welles left it up to the audience to digest and order the facts that he presented, beginning with the great man's death and the press newsreel of his life.

'News on the March,' an extraordinarily convincing piece of film editing, is a newsreel segment on the life of Charles Foster Kane, designed to give the viewer a neat, allegedly complete and fact-filled chronological encapsulation of the newspaperman's life. Beginning with '1941's biggest and strangest' funeral, Kane's coffin emerges from Xanadu into the sunshine while rousing music accompanies the footage of Kane's palatial home, Xanadu. A male narrator ticks off the inventory of Kane's life. Referring to Kane as 'America's Kubla Khan,' the narrator rattles off statistics about Xanadu—the largest monument to one person since the pyramids of the Egyptian Pharaohs, which houses the 'biggest private zoo since Noah'—and continues in that vein as Kane's priceless collections of art are paraded across the screen.

To most people, Xanadu represents the castle that newspaper mogul William Randolph Hearst built in San Simeon, California for his mistress, the actress Marion Davies. Hearst's patronage of actress Marion Davies is an obvious source of inspiration for Kane's affair with Susan Alexander. Unlike Kane's affair with Susan, however, which culminated in marriage and ended in divorce, the Hearst-Davies affair was sincere and lasting. Had Mrs Hearst consented to a divorce, William and Marion would almost certainly have married.

Davies was said to be an accomplished comedic actress who might have acheived stardom without the help of Hearst, whose excessive publicity for all of Davies' vehicles worked more to her *disadvantage* at the box office. Despite her natural aptitude at comedy and gutsy roles, Hearst wanted her to play fragile and virginal characters.

Right: Agnes Moorehead joined Orson Welles' Mercury Theater Company in 1940. Her illustrious career spanned 57 years and she was nominated five times for Academy Awards.

Hearst formed a production company, Cosmopolitan Pictures, solely for launching Davies to film stardom. In 1924, he moved the company under the wing of the Goldwyn Company, and it was included in the Metro-Goldwyn-Mayer merger. As a result of her lack of box-office success and the pre-war depression of the 1930s, she and Hearst lost a considerable amount of money. Finally, with the advent of talkies, Davies was offered fewer roles because she spoke with a slight stutter.

Another possible source for the Susan character may have been Hearst's first love, an opera singer named Sybil Sanderson who died in her late thirties, ruined by alcoholism, poor health and scandal.

Albeit, the name Susan Alexander actually was inspired by Welles' screenplay typist.

The cast was hand-picked by Welles from his 'on Broadway' Mercury Theater Company, which he co-founded with John Houseman in 1937. The virtually unknown cast included Orson Welles, Joseph Cotten, Dorothy Comingore, Agnes Moorehead, Ruth Warrick, Ray Collins, Erksine Sanford, Everett Sloane, William Alland, Paul Stewart and George Coulouris. Most of the actors had little or no prior experience in front of a camera. Had they been seasoned *film* actors, it is doubtful that Welles' unconventional production would have gotten off the ground. Few 'stars' were willing to trust their reputations to an inexperienced director like Welles.

In preparation for actual production, Welles and his cast and crew studied the most significant footage the studio had to offer, and experimented with lights, cameras, microphones and cranes. In just one year, the script for **Citizen Kane** was written, the actors learned to move naturally in front of a camera, and all production work was completed. Only four months was spent filming.

The end result is an enduring and meticulously produced film that merits distinction for its unique treatment of biography and parody. Still inspiring generations of film lovers after 50 years, **Citizen Kane** is, without a doubt, a classic of the first order of magnitude.

Right: Orson Welles: actor, writer, director, producer.

CITIZEN KANE

Right: Orson Welles was born in Kenosha, Wisconsin on 6 May 1915. The second son of Richard and Beatrice Welles, Orson had a happy, though irregular, childhood. Orson grew up in an atmosphere of creativity and eccentricity. Educated at home, he showed aptitude at drama, poetry, cartooning, piano and magic.

Overleaf: In a flashback of Kane's childhood, we see the moment Charles Foster Kane, as a small boy, meets Walter Parks Thatcher, his new legal guardian and bank manager. 'Come on, Charles. Let's shake hands. Now, now! I'm not as frightening as all that! Let's shake, what do you say?'
The young Kane, played by Buddy Swan, was suspicious of the stuffy young man who came to his mother's boarding house. Thatcher, played by George Coulouris, was summoned in secret by Mrs Kane. From a defaulting boarder she received the supposedly worthless deed to an abandoned mine shaft. Ultimately, however, the Colorado Lode proved to be the third richest gold mine in the world!
As the sole owner, Mrs Kane signed over total control to the bank with the stipulations that $50,000 a year go to the Kanes for their lifetimes and that the rest remain in a trust fund for the boy until he reached 25 years of age, at which time he would come into complete possession.

Above: A behind-the-scenes shot of Thatcher, Mrs Kane and the boy at the moment when Thatcher and the boy meet for the first time. Welles is to the left of the camera with his pipe clamped tightly between his teeth.

The photographic effects in **Citizen Kane** were thoroughly planned in advance and Welles had virtually every scene drawn out on storyboards, in much the same way that Alfred Hitchcock worked.

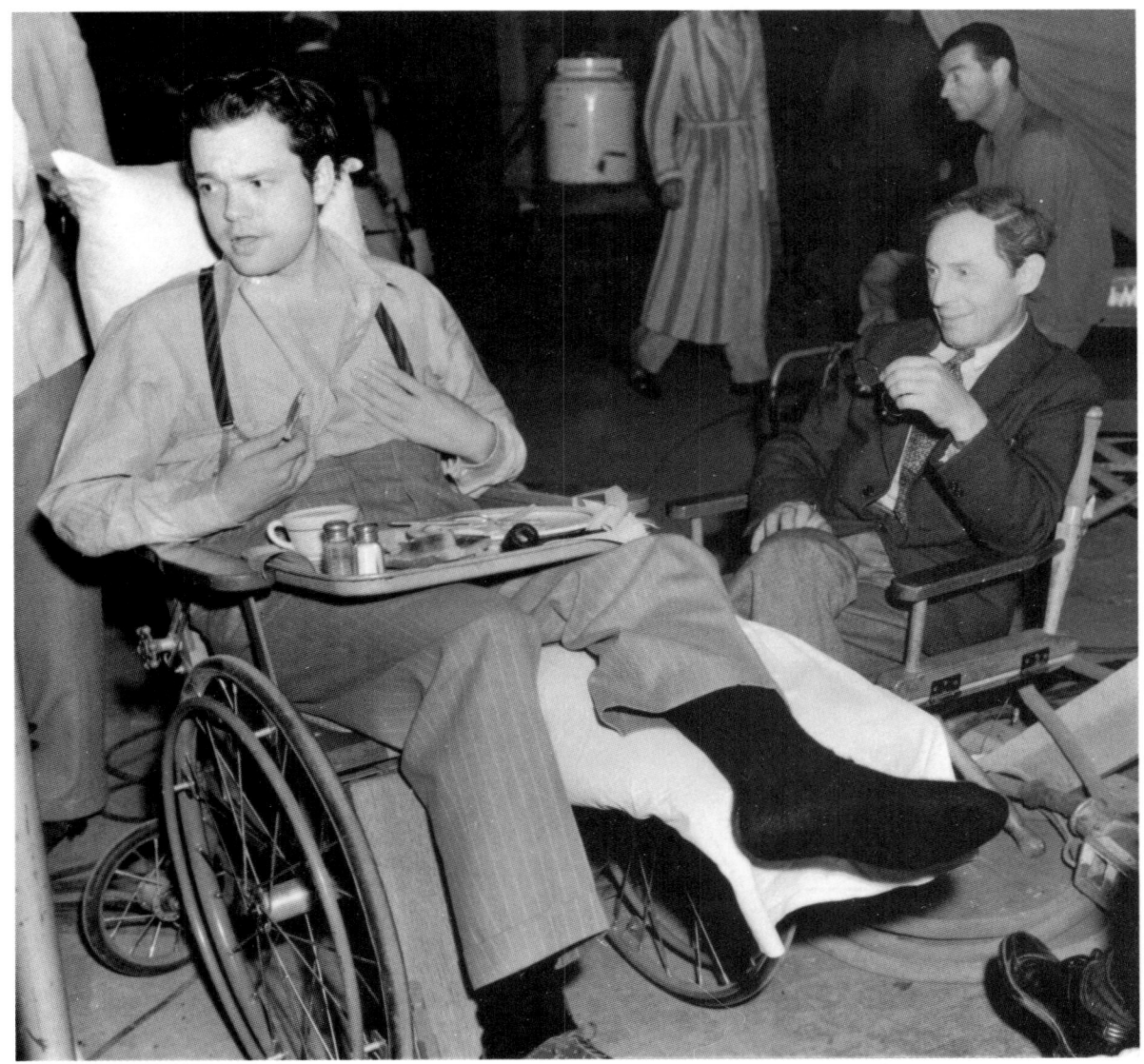

Above: Two weeks ahead of the filming schedule, Orson broke his ankle during the scene in which Kane chases Gettys down the stairs of Susan Alexander's apartment the night before the election. Since Welles would not be able to reshoot the scene until his ankle healed, Joseph Cotten was called in to do his part as the 70-year-old Jedediah Leland who is interviewed on the rooftop solarium of the hospital by Thompson, the reporter. Wheelchair to wheelchair, Welles directed Cotten in his biggest scene in **Citizen Kane**.

To Orson's left is friend and mentor Dr Maurice Bernstein. He was Welles' legal guardian after the death of his parents. Orson invited him to Hollywood from Chicago to attend to his ankle and possibly to get Bernstein a job as 'doctor to the stars.'

Right: Jedediah Leland (right) and Charlie Kane (left) arrive at the offices of the *Inquirer* in a hansom cab dressed as New York dandies. It is the summer of 1892.

'Take a good look at it Jed,' Kane said. 'It's going to look a lot different one of these days.'

Above: Erskine Sanford played the obsequious Mr Herbert Carter. In this scene, after mistaking Leland for Kane, Carter welcomes Kane to the *Inquirer*. Carter, the paper's senior editor, has definite ideas about how a 'respectable' paper should be run. He is totally unprepared for the changes Kane has in mind for the *Inquirer*.

Left: A promotional photo of Joseph Cotten dressed in his wardrobe for the scenes of his first day at the *Inquirer*, where Kane appoints him dramatic critic.

'I hope I haven't made a mistake, Jedediah. It *is* dramatic critic you want to be, isn't it?'

Above: Welles steps out of character to give direction during Kane's first day at the *Inquirer*.

Gregg Toland, seated behind the camera, agreed with Welles that shooting an indoor scene with a visible ceiling contributes to a more realistic picture. The false ceilings such as the one in this still reflected light more naturally than a ceilingless sound stage, and provided the perfect foil for overhead microphones as well.

Right: 'Orson Welles, Genius' this self-assured portrait seems to say. Nicknamed 'the wonder boy' by Nelson Rockefeller, Welles gained a reputation as a flamboyant and highly creative actor, writer, director and producer.

At a young age, Orson showed an aptitude for drama and poetry. His parents Richard and Beatrice Welles encouraged his artistic pursuits and held company with talented musicians, artists and inventors of the day. His father was a capricious inventor who was prone to smoking and drinking and had a great love of the theater.

Beatrice was an accomplished concert pianist, and was often hosting parties for celebrities from the entertainment and art world like Ravel and Stravinsky. An outspoken advocate for women's rights, she was an eloquent speaker. Beatrice died of hepatitis when Orson was eight. His father then eased into full-time parenting by taking him on a tour of Jamaica and the Far East.

Orson was enrolled in the Todd School in Illinois at age 11, and graduated in 1931. Instead of college he went to Dublin for a year and tried unsuccessfully to break onto the London stage. He returned to New York where he was snubbed by Broadway. In 1932 he left the country again, this time for Morocco and Spain, where he wrote a few popular detective stories which were sold to American magazines for a nominal fee. In Seville he poured over Hemingway's *Death in the Afternoon,* and as a result, Orson himself began a brief and undistinguished career as a bullfighter.

In 1933 he returned to the United States and won the role of Mercutio in Katherine Cornell's company production of *Romeo and Juliet.* The following year he gave his first radio performance, a four-minute short called *The Hearts of Age,* which he co-directed.

In 1937 Orson Welles and John Houseman founded the Mercury Theater, which soon became known for its bold and innovative productions. The company transferred its creative energies to radio in 1938 and 'The Mercury Theater on the Air' gained instant acclaim for its realistic broadcast of HG Wells' *War of the Worlds.* The broadcast so terrified listeners in New Jersey that many evacuated their homes, fearing a hostile alien invasion.

Previous pages: Kane has already made himself at home in Carter's private sanctum, much to the disgruntled editor's dismay. Leland and Bernstein (Everett Sloane) are looking at the headline of the *Chronicle*: 'Brooklyn Woman Missing!'

'Now look, Mr Carter, here's a front-page story in the *Chronicle* about a Mrs Harry Silverstone in Brooklyn who's missing. Now, she's probably murdered. Here's a picture of her in the *Chronicle*. Why isn't there something like it in the *Inquirer*?' Kane asks.

Left: Indignant Carter sputters, 'It's not our function to report the gossip of housewives. If we were interested in that kind of thing, Mr Kane, we could fill the paper twice over daily.'

'… [T]hat's the kind of thing we are going to be interested in from now on!'

Above: 'We'll be on the street soon, Charlie, another 10 minutes,' says Jed, looking out at the *Chronicle* newsboy crying the headline.

'Three hours and 50 minutes late, but we did it,' Bernstein chimes in.

Above: After making over the paper four times in one night, Kane turns and faces Bernstein and Leland with his just completed 'Declaration of Principles':

'I'll provide the people of this city with a daily paper that will tell all the news honestly. I will also provide them with a fighting and tireless champion of their rights as citizens and as human beings. Signed, Charles Foster Kane, The Publisher.'

Kane asked the typesetter, Solly, to remake the front page to include his 'Declaration of Principles' as a boxed item on the front page. Leland stops Solly and requests that the original of Kane's 'Declaration' be returned to him after he's done with it. Leland senses the significance of the document and wants to keep it:

'I've got a hunch it might turn out to be one of the important papers of our time… .like the Declaration of Independence, and the Constitution, and my first report card at school.'

Left and above: A proud and tired Kane and Leland are standing in the center of a pile of *Inquirer*s. These two promotional photos were taken immediately before the final scene was filmed. In the film's final version, the camera shows a close-up of the front page and gradually pulls back to reveal stacks of newspapers. Hands then come into the frame and remove the stacks.

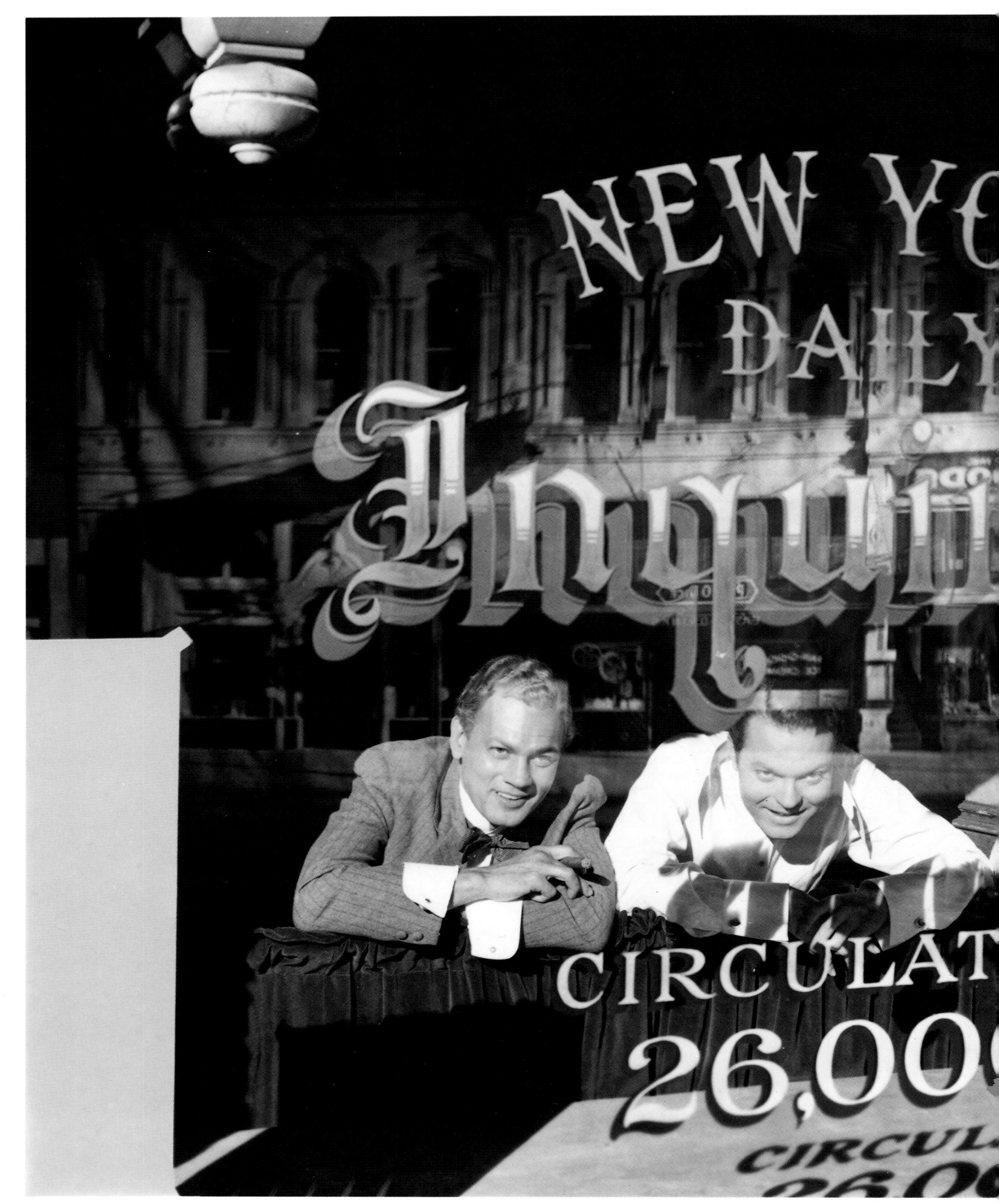

After the long night, Kane, Leland and Bernstein watch as newsboys start hawking the morning *Inquirer*. The plate glass window in this scene shows the paper's circulation is a meager 26,000.

A dissolve shows the three staring glumly in front of the *Chronicle*'s window. The rival paper's circulation is at 495,000, and a portrait of nine of the best journalists returns the men's gaze.

Another dissolve shows the same nine men in a second portrait, this time with Kane, front row, center. The camera pulls back and it becomes evident that the journalists are now part of the *Inquirer* staff and this is their reception.

'Welcome, gentlemen, to the *Inquirer*. It will make you happy to learn that our circulation this moring was the greatest in New York... 684,132.'

Left: A large ice sculpture in the shape of a 'K' bears a front page headline that welcomes the new staff to the *Inquirer*. Kane has just bought the staff that took 20 years for the *Chronicle* to assemble. Six years ago, like a kid in a candy store, he looked at their portrait in the *Chronicle* window, and *now*, six years later, Kane has his candy. He doesn't pretend to want their loyalty; he wants their combined talents to make the *Inquirer* the best paper in the world.

The party takes place in the city room of the *Inquirer* at 1:30 am one evening in 1898.

Overleaf: Kane and Bernstein (at the foot of the table) banter about Kane's promises to his doctor, his upcoming vacation and his penchant for collecting statues.

'—You can't blame me, Mr Bernstein. They've been making statues for two thousand years, and I've only been buying for five.'

'—Promise me, Mr Kane.'

'I promise you, Mr Bernstein.'

'Thank you.'

'Oh, Mr Bernstein—you don't expect me to keep any of my promises, do you?'

Right: Carved in ice are caricatures of Bernstein and Kane. The party is underway and everyone is enjoying himself. Even Leland manages to laugh, despite his disapproval of Kane's warmongering:

'Well, gentlemen, are we going to declare war on Spain?'

'The *Inquirer* already has,' comes Leland's terse reply.

This exchange is a reference to the 1898 political situation that William Randolph Hearst was encouraging and supporting with constant coverage: the emerging Spanish-American War. Hearst has been credited with having sent writer Richard Harding Davis and artist Frederic Remington to Cuba to 'cover' the war which had not yet begun. Remington supposedly cabled Hearst that there was no war. As the story goes, Hearst cabled back saying, 'Remington, Havana. Please remain. You furnish the pictures and I'll furnish the war. WR Hearst.'

Whether these words were authored by Hearst is inconclusive, however. The implication was made in **Citizen Kane** that Kane, a thinly disguised Hearst, had fomented the American public into a state of outrage. Just as Kane corrects *Inquirer* editor Carter, '—[I]f the headline is big enough, it makes the news big enough'—Hearst papers fabricated stories of the war before the United States actually became involved.

When the American battleship, the USS *Maine*, was blown up in the Havana harbor on 15 February 1898, killing 260 men, the battle cry 'Remember the *Maine*' was on everyone's lips thanks to Hearst's headlines. On 24 April the United States declared war on Spain.

Previous pages: Welles issues stage directions during a rehearsal of the 'dancing girls' scene. The girls' costumes resemble soldiers' uniforms, in keeping with Kane's interest in the growing conflict with Spain.

These pages: The center of attention, Kane has joined the chorus girls in a song and dance routine:
    'I'll bet you five you're not alive
    If you don't know his name.
    What is his name?
    It's Charlie Kane.
    It's Mister Kane.
    He doesn't like that Mister
    He likes good old Charlie Kane.'

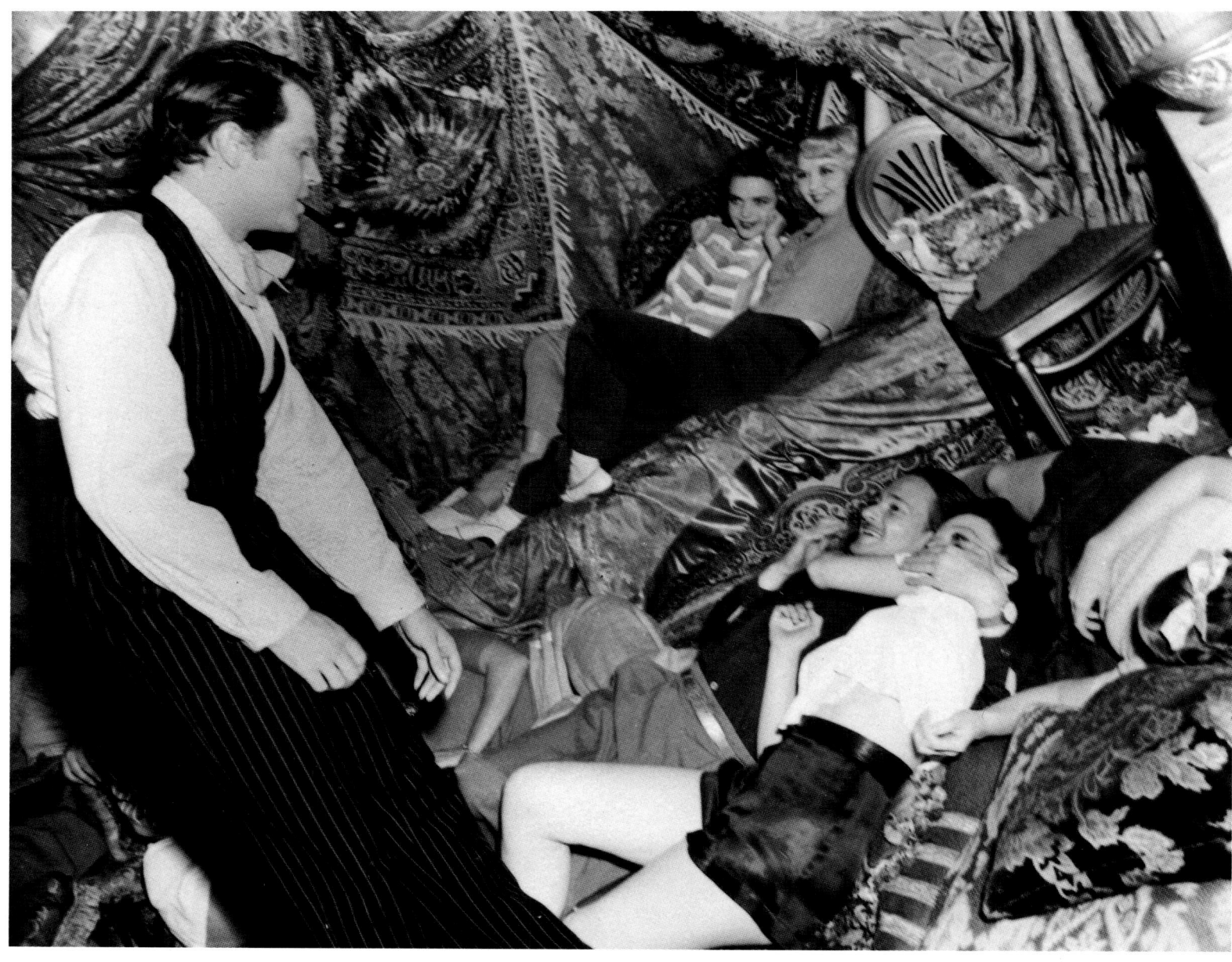

Above: Orson Welles directs a scene set in a *fin de siècle* brothel that was ultimately cut from **Citizen Kane**. The original screenplay was censored by the Production Code Office for depicting Georgie as a madam and for setting a scene in her brothel. The general climate in pre-World War II Hollywood is evident in this excerpt from a letter from Joseph I Breen to RKO on 15 July 1940:

'There should be nothing in this scene which indicates that Georgie is a "madam" or that the girls brought into the party are prostitutes. This flavor should be very carefully guarded against.'

The scene introducing Georgie had to be rewritten, eliminating Georgie completely and replacing the prostitutes with dancing girls.

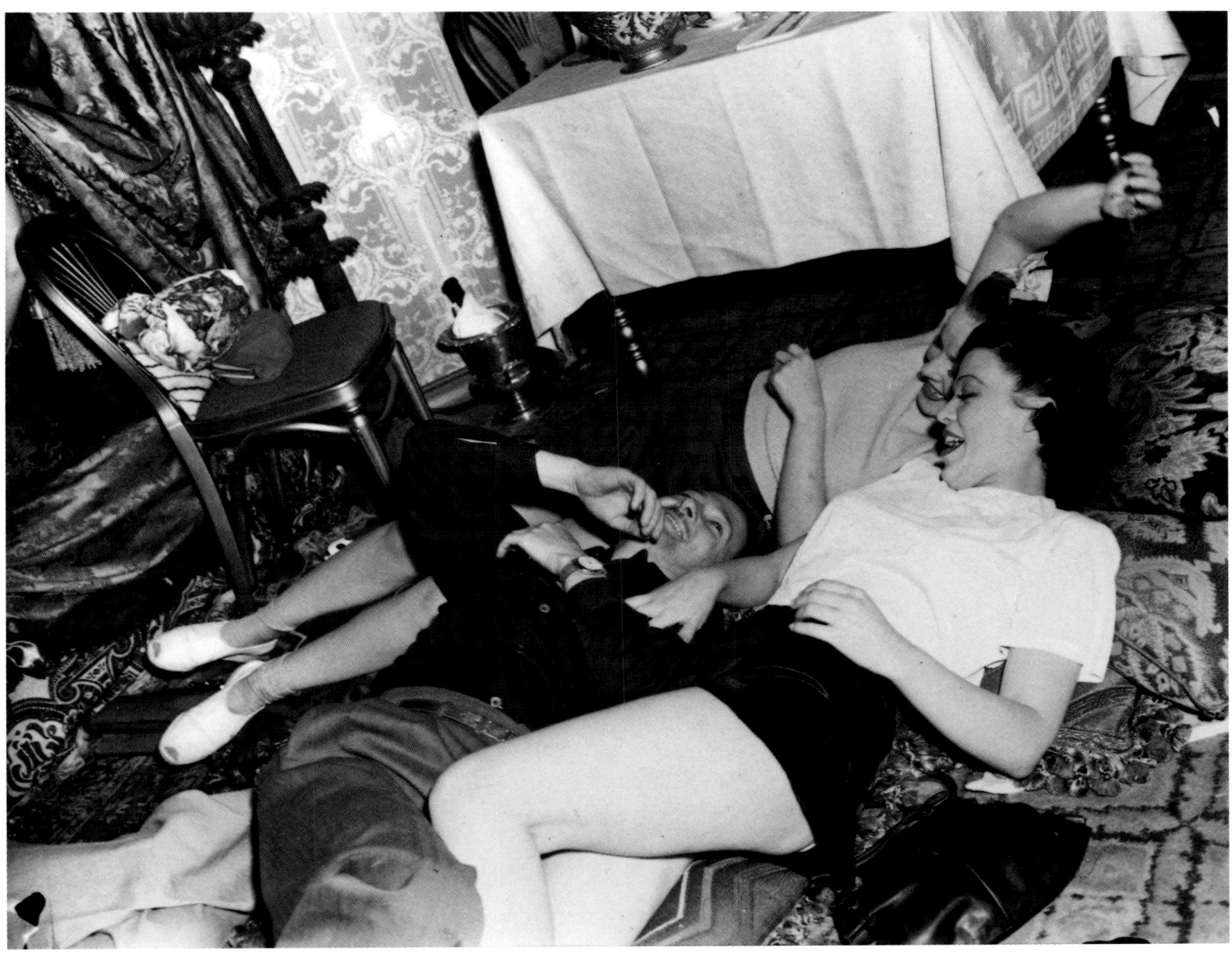

Above: This fun-loving rehearsal for the bordello scene in **Citizen Kane** would never pass the censors at the Production Code Office, as Breen explained in his letter:

'There is one important detail in the story at hand which is quite definitely in violation of the Production Code and, consequently, cannot be approved. This is the locale set down for scene 64, which is, inescapably, a brothel. Please have in mind that there is a specific regulation in the Production Code which prohibits the exhibition of brothels.

'In all the circumstances, we suggest that the locale in this scene be changed and that there be nothing about the playing of the scene which would suggest that the place is a brothel.'

In the final version, Georgie's character and the bordello scene were deleted from the script.

CK-70

Left: While Kane travels abroad, Leland and Bernstein remain at the *Inquirer* unpacking and storing the sculptures he sends back for his collection. In this scene Bernstein has just read a telegram from Kane, who is in Paris and planning to buy the world's largest diamond. Bernstein gathers that instead of collecting statues, 'he's collecting somebody that's collecting diamonds.'

Everett Sloane, who plays Bernstein in **Citizen Kane**, turned to acting after he lost his job as a Wall Street runner in the stock market crash of 1929. He appeared on stage and in numerous radio dramas, making his Broadway debut in 1935. Soon after, he joined the Mercury Theater and followed Welles to Hollywood, hoping to get into screen acting. He gave powerful performances in Welles' **The Lady From Shanghai** (1948) and in Fielder Cook's **Patterns** (1956), and shared the screen with Welles in Norman Foster's **Journey Into Fear** (1943).

Previous pages: This scene still shows a dapper Kane's return from Europe. The staff at the *Inquirer* has presented him with a large winner's cup that reads: 'Welcome Home Mr Kane.' His distracted appearance is soon explained when the social announcement that Kane handed Miss Townsend (far right) is read out loud.

'Mr and Mrs Thomas Monroe Norton announce the engagement of their daughter, Emily Monroe Norton, to Mr Charles Foster Kane.'

Left: The happy couple pose for photographers on the back lawn of the White House after their wedding. Emily Monroe Norton, niece to the President, is played by Ruth Warrick. This scene was shown in the 'News on the March' newsreel as well as during Leland's recollection of Kane's marriage to Emily. Of the marriage Leland recalls,

'... [A]fter the first couple of months they never saw much of each other except at breakfast. It was a marriage just like any other marriage.'

Overleaf: Very much in love, Kane and Emily have just returned from a night of parties. Living in the fast lane is new for Emily, who has never stayed up all night and is worried what the servants will think.

Above: The disintegration of Kane's first marriage is vividly depicted in just six scenes which take place at the breakfast table. Welles made the glimpses of their private life believable with succinct dialogue and by limiting the technical effects to changes in lighting, the special effects outside the window, the food and the wardrobe.

Previous page: In each of the six scenes in the breakfast montage, Emily and Kane gradually are seated further away from each other at the table, emphasizing the breakdown of their relationship over the course of nine years.

Neither Emily nor the grapefruit, however, appeared in **Citizen Kane** as they are in this wardrobe test photo.

Left: A close-up of Kane in 1909, taken from the final scene of the breakfast sequence.

In the first year of marriage, Emily shows signs of resenting the *Inquirer*'s demands on Kane's time, and he responds, 'You never should have married a newspaperman. They're worse than sailors.'

Kane's public and private criticism of the president bothers Emily, who sees the office of the president as a sacred cow. Kane's attacks on the president are representative of Hearst's condemnation of McKinley's reluctance to wage war against Spain. Hearst's brand of journalism kept alive American pro-war sentiments. The loss of the *Maine* and public pressure spurred McKinley to action and he demanded Spain's withdrawal from Cuba. Despite the concessions made by Spain, on 21 April 1898 war was declared by an act of Congress.

In the fourth scene, which takes place in their sixth year of marriage, Emily and Kane disagree over a gift that Bernstein gave to their son. When she questions whether Bernstein has to visit the nursery at all, Kane snaps a 'Yes' that ends debate on that subject and closes the scene.

Overleaf: In the last breakfast scenario there is no verbal exchange between Kane and Emily. Each sits at opposite ends of the table reading the paper. Kane reads the *Inquirer*, while Emily, in silent protest, reads the *Chronicle*.

Left: Kane was on his way to make 'a sort of sentimental journey' to the Western Manhattan Warehouse containing the things from his mother's house in New Salem, Colorado, when a passing carriage splashed him with mud.

Above: Susan Alexander (Dorothy Comingore) has just left the drugstore where she had a prescription filled for a toothache. It hurts her very much, but seeing Kane covered in mud she can't keep herself from laughing at him.

An amused Susan offers Kane some hot water from her apartment behind them. Kane accepts and a platonic relationship develops. Learning that Susan's mother had dreams of her becoming an opera singer, Kane becomes the patron of her opera career.

Above: Kane has taken on mythic proportions as 'the fighting liberal, and the friend of the workingman.' Leland has been outside Madison Square Garden boosting support for Kane while inside Kane assures the workingman and the slum child, that 'the decent, ordinary citizens know I'll do everything in my power to protect the underprivileged, the underpaid, and the underfed.'

Right: Kane is the center of attention in this famous photo as he makes his campaign speech on the eve of the gubernatorial election.

These famous photos emphasize the power and commanding presence of Kane and Welles as Charles Foster Kane. The set and the camera angles together were designed to make Kane appear larger than life, a hero to the underclass.

Left: Captivated by the grand spectacle of Kane's election speech and the enthusiastic crowd, son and wife are swept away by his words to protect and serve the workingman and see that slum children do not go hungry:

   'Mom, is Pop governor yet?'

   'Not yet, Junior.'

Left: In addition to numerous attacks on his opponent, the incumbent, Jim W Gettys, in the *Inquirer*, he makes a final promise to his supporters at the Garden:

'But here's one promise I'll make, and Boss Jim Gettys knows I'll keep it. My first offical act as governor of this state will be to appoint a special district attorney to arrange for the indictment, prosecution and conviction of Boss Jim W Gettys.'

Above: Jim Gettys, played by Ray Collins, has been listening to Kane's campaign speech unseen from a balcony. As the crowd roars with applause and rousing band music begins, Gettys turns and puts on his hat, off to a rendezvous armed with very potent ammunition to put an end to Kane's attacks.

Having just delivered the speech that would surely convince the undecided that Charles Foster Kane is the best man for governor, Kane is given an enthusiastic welcome by Junior and Emily *(left)*.

Kane will not, however, win the election as his son expects. Instead he will forfeit the election and his marriage, because his self-obsession will ultimately prevail over good sense and good advice from Gettys, Emily and Susan.

Overleaf: Emily has sent Junior home with the chauffeur and wants Charles to accompany her by taxi to 185 West 74th Street, the home of Susan Alexander.

Ruth Warrick infused the part of Emily with the self-possessed dignity Welles wanted to be evident in the role of Kane's first wife. As niece to the president, Emily carried herself with the propriety one would expect of a member of the American royal family. Her morals beyond reproach, Emily and Junior were victims of Kane's unscrupulousness.

When they arrive at Susan's apartment, Kane is welcomed by name by the maid, 'Come right in, Mr Kane.' Her familiarity leads the audience and Emily to suspect that more than a platonic relationship exists between Kane and Susan. Although the scene is over in a matter of seconds, the tension between Kane and Emily is high as Emily stiffly enters the building with Kane following like a whipped dog.

Right: Waiting upstairs is an apprehensive Susan and Boss Jim Gettys.

'Charlie... Charlie, he forced me to send your wife that letter. I didn't want to. He's been saying the most terrible—'

Realizing he was trapped, Kane turns his anger on Gettys and threatens to break his neck. Emily's calm voice of reason keeps her in command of the situation, and this infuriates Kane.

'Charles. Your breaking this man's neck would hardly explain this note.'

Above: Emily received an anonymous note that reads: 'Serious consequences for Mr Kane, for yourself and for your son.'

'What does this mean, Miss—?'

Susan introduces herself and admits that she wrote the note, but only after Gettys threatened her with a smear campaign against her and Kane.

Above: Susan begs Charlie to listen to reason: 'Charlie, you got other things to think about. Your little boy, you don't want him to read about you in the papers.'

Gettys has offered Kane a choice, to withdraw from the race or face certain political death. 'Unless Mr Kane makes up his mind by tomorrow that he's so sick he has to go away for a year or two, Monday morning every paper in this state, except his, will carry the story I'm going to give them.'

The story, of course, is that Kane's secret extra-marital relationship with Susan Alexander proves that his private life is incompatible with his public image of a man on a moral crusade to clean up his state.

Without considering the consequences his actions will have on his family, his professional reputation or Susan, Kane has made his decision to stay with Susan and face a public scandal.

Left: In one of the most famous scenes in **Citizen Kane**, the protagonist chases Gettys down the stairs of Susan's apartment shouting, 'Gettys, I'm going to send you to Sing Sing. Sing Sing, Gettys. Sing Sing.'

Welles broke his ankle shooting this scene and was wheelchair bound for several weeks.

Above: Emily waits outside for her ride as Gettys, fleeing Kane's insults, prepares to open the door. That fateful night in 1916, Emily left Charles with Susan, and her last words were 'You decided what you were going to do, Charles, some time ago.'

Two years later, Emily and their son were killed in an automobile accident.

Left: An ardent Kane supporter, Jedediah Leland, comes to the campaign headquarters drunk the day after the election. The *Chronicle* headline reads:

**CANDIDATE KANE CAUGHT IN LOVE NEST
WITH 'SINGER'**

while the *Inquirer*'s reads:

**CHARLES FOSTER KANE DEFEATED
FRAUD AT POLLS!**

Disillusioned and disgusted by Kane's lack of presence in assuming that the people would vote for him over Gettys despite the scandal, Jedediah launches into Kane:

'You talk about the people as though you owned them. As though they belong to you.... You remember the workingman? He's turning into something called organized labor. You're not going to like that one bit when you find out it means your workingman expects something as his right and not your gift....

'You don't care about anything except you. You just want to persuade people that you love them so much that they ought to love you back. Only you want love on your own terms.'

Leland asks to be transferred out of town to the Chicago paper. Kane protests but gives in when Leland offers to resign.

'A toast, Jedediah, to love on my terms. Those are the only terms anybody ever knows.'

Left: As the newlyweds Kane and Susan come down the stairs they are swamped by photographers. Kane, armed with an umbrella, forces his way through the crowd to a waiting carriage. One battered photographer calls out, 'Hey, Mr Kane, I'm from the *Inquirer*,' to which Kane responds, 'Huh? All right, fire away, boys. I used to be a reporter myself.'

When asked if he was through with politics, Kane replied, 'I would say vice versa,' implying that politics was through with him.

Having married Susan, he turned his energies toward making a success out of her since he'd failed at making a success of himself. 'We're going to be a great opera star,' Kane tells the reporters.

Already Kane is speaking for Susan and telling her what she will have and not asking her what she desires for herself. It is this trait that will eventually drive Susan away from Kane.

Overleaf: In preparation for the scene of Susan's operatic debut, Orson Welles (in the wheelchair) and Gregg Toland (standing at the camera) check Dorothy Comingore's position (left). Her cues are written on the chalkboard next to the camera.

Left: Susan opens the new Chicago Opera House with her debut performance in *Salammbô*. Backstage before the curtain rises, the scene is one of general confusion: people are rushing around taking their places; final arrangements are made to Susan's costume; her voice coach, Signor Matisti (played by real life opera singer Fortunio Bonanova), gives Susan last minute instruction; and the people around her are wringing their hands anxiously.

Welles was a strong opponent of the close-up and used them sparingly. At Susan's debut, however, a super close-up of Susan's terrified face and tear-filled eyes as she sings effectively conveys her terror and prompts the audience to feel pity for the diva. But there is an undeniably comedic current in the grandiose production.

As her thin voice rises pathetically from the stage, the camera moves up into the rafters high above the stage to a catwalk. There, two stage hands are listening to Susan's aria and one gives his colorful opinion of her singing by pinching his nose.

The scene of Susan's debut is retold to Thompson twice, once by Leland and once by Susan. In Susan's recollection, Kane is depicted as a dictator who, for his own reasons, responds as if the bad reviews of Susan's singing are a reflection on *his* character. Using Susan as a pawn in his efforts to save face, Kane orders Susan to continue singing, as if it were *he* who was personally humiliated by the bad reviews.

In Susan's words, 'You don't propose to have *yourself* made ridiculous! What about me? I'm the one that's got to do the singing. I'm the one that gets the razzberries.'

Above: Welles rehearses Kane's one-man standing ovation for Susan.

The night of the opera Kane is in the audience. He has overheard a woman making disparaging remarks about Susan's performance, 'Perfectly dreadful... .'

At the end of the final act the audience gives weak applause but Kane stands applauding loudly until he realizes the house lights are already on and people are getting up to leave.

Left: Charles Foster Kane has just returned from Susan's operatic debut at the new Chicago Opera House that Kane had built for her. He enters the darkened *Inquirer* offices and overhears the men who have been designated the task of reviewing Susan's miserable performance in *Salammbô*.

In keeping with Kane's self-aggrandizing coverage of events, they've covered all angles—news, social, music, dramatic—to the point of excess. 'Everything has been done exactly to your instructions, Mr Kane. We've got two spreads of pictures and—'

The reviews are naturally enthusiastic, but Kane knows that one is missing: Jedediah Leland's review on the dramatic merits of Susan's debut.

The only outstanding review of Susan's debut is Leland's, who was to cover the performance's dramatic merits. Seen making paper dolls out of his program during the opera, Leland promptly got drunk afterward.

Kane finds him slumped over his typewriter *(right)*, the unfinshed review still in the typewriter. Too inebriated to finish his own critique, Kane finishes it for Leland, in the style of the first few lines:

'Miss Susan Alexander, a pretty but hopelessly incompetent amateur, last night opened the new Chicago Opera House in a performance of *Salammbô*. Her singing, happily, is no concern of this department. Of her acting, it is absolutely impossible to—'

When Leland finds out that Kane is finishing his notice, he wrongly assumes that Charlie is 'fixing it up.' Leland is fired on the spot, and from Susan we learn that he was given a check for $25,000 as a parting gesture from Kane.

As a struggling actor, Joseph Cotten held odd jobs and wrote occasional dramatic reviews for the Miami *Herald* before he went to Broadway in the 1930s and worked under David Belasco as stage manager and understudy. Joseph Cotten met Orson Welles in 1935 while both were rehearsing a radio broadcast. In 1936 Cotten was cast in the part of Freddy in an Orson Welles production of the satirical *Horse Eats Hat*.

In 1937 he joined the Mercury Theater, and a year later he played the lead in a 40-minute film produced by Welles and John Houseman that would be inserted in a stage version of *Too Much Johnson*. No prints of this film are known to exist, the last copy having been destroyed in a 1970 fire at Welles' villa in Madrid.

Cotten's good looks and acting ability earned him the lead opposite Katherine Hepburn in the Broadway play *The Philadelphia Story* (1939). His reputation as a leading man was well established when Welles called Cotten to Hollywood, offering him the part of Jedediah Leland in **Citizen Kane**. Leland was Kane's friend from college who had been given a job as the *Inquirer*'s dramatic critic.

Cotten would return to work under Welles' direction in **The Magnificent Ambersons** (1942) and **Journey into Fear** (1942), **Othello** (1952), a cameo in **A Touch of Evil** (1958), **F for Fake** (1973) and with Welles in Carol Reed's **The Third Man** (1949). Under Hitchcock he played in **Shadow of a Doubt** (1943) and **Under Capricorn** (1949). In 1948 he won the Best Actor Award at the Venice Festival for his performance in **Portrait of Jennie**.

Previous pages: The Great Depression has enveloped the country's economy and even Kane feels its cripling effect. Kane has relinquished control of his newspapers and syndicates to Thatcher and Company.

Once again Kane is Thatcher's charge, dependent on him for all material things.

Above: A bored Susan sits in Xanadu's great hall doing jigsaw puzzles to pass the time.

Left: Kane's distant voice echoes across the huge room as he approaches the table where Susan is working her puzzle. She wants to leave Xanadu and go to New York.

'A person could go crazy in this dump. Nobody to talk to, nobody to have any fun with.'

Kane, who looks to be standing *in* the enormous fireplace answers: 'Our home is here, Susan. I don't want to go to New York.'

Before Susan abandoned her operatic career she attempted suicide, but Kane refused to believe that she would want to leave his world.

Despite all the rare and priceless things present in Xanadu—the fine art that decorates the castle, the world's largest private zoo on the castle grounds—Susan feels that Kane has never given her anything she *really* cares about. The tension that has been building between Kane and Susan explodes on their picnic. A black musician is singing 'It can't be love' while Kane and Susan argue:

'You never gave me anything in your life. You just tried to buy me into giving you something.'

'Whatever I do, I do because I love you.'

'You don't love me. You want me to love you. Sure, I'm Charles Foster Kane,' Susan mimicks. 'Whatever you want, just name it and it's yours. But you gotta love me.'

At that, Kane slaps Susan hard across the mouth.

'Don't tell me you're sorry.'

'I'm not sorry,' is Kane's frosty reply.

Left: Kane has gone to Susan's room at her request. He realizes that she is about to leave him. Her bags are packed and she's sent for the car. Now all that remains is to say good-bye.

In this behind-the-scenes photo, we are privy to the elaborate sets constructed for **Citizen Kane**. While Welles rehearses on stage, the cameramen are postioned below the level of the stage. From this vantage point the camera, with the deep focus lenses devised by Gregg Toland, can follow Kane, and at the same time keep the entire room in focus.

The idea for constructing ceilinged sets lends itself to scenes like this. Inevitably the ceiling will enter the field of vision in this oblique view. Shooting from the floor enhances the stature of the actor and is a perspective that was employed repeatedly for Welles' screen appearances.

Left: Susan has made up her mind to leave. Kane wonders if she's gone completely crazy.

Above: When he sees that she's serious, he begins to beg: 'Please don't go. Please, Susan. From now on, everything will be exactly the way you want it to be, not the way I *think* you want it, but *your* way, Susan....'

Previous pages: 'You mustn't go. You can't do this to me,' Kane pleads.

'I see, it's you that this is being done to. It's not me at all. Not what it means to me. I can't do this to you. Oh, yes, I can.'

Above: Thompson, the reporter, has followed Susan's suggestion of questioning Raymond, the butler, regarding the possible meaning of 'Rosebud.' Raymond, played by Paul Stewart, is a self-serving individual who offers to tell Thompson what he knows for a fee: one thousand dollars. Raymond doesn't have the answer to the mystery surrounding 'Rosebud,' but he shows Thompson the vast treasures that Kane amassed over his lifetime.

Thompson realizes that knowing the meaning of 'Rosebud,' the last word on Kane's lips, 'wouldn't have explained anything. I don't think any word can explain a man's life. No, I guess Rosebud is just a piece in a jigsaw puzzle, a missing piece.'

Above: Welles is seated at the center of the photo behind the camera. The camera is mounted on tracks that allow the camera to follow the action and movements of the actors. Approximately 144 wooden cases and packing crates were collected for this scene.

Left: Welles had nine different sets of false teeth and implants made to change his appearance and facial structure in order to simulate the human aging process. Here he is made-up as a nearly 70-year-old Kane.

Above: Orson Welles at the pinnacle of his film career, in costume for **Citizen Kane**. In 1975, Orson Welles was finally honored by the people in the film industry who for so long had spurned him. These were people who refused to work with him, neglected to consider him for acting roles, or finance his films, yet they all recognized his influence on Hollywood and cinema. The third person ever to receive it, Welles accepted the Life Achievement Award of the American Film Institute.

INDEX